Submission to Divin in the Death of ⎯⎯⎯⎯

Recommended and inforced, in a sermon preached at Northampton, on the death of a very amiable and hopeful child, about five years old

Philip Doddridge

Alpha Editions

This edition published in 2024

ISBN : 9789364735971

Design and Setting By
Alpha Editions
www.alphaedis.com
Email - info@alphaedis.com

As per information held with us this book is in Public Domain.
This book is a reproduction of an important historical work. Alpha Editions uses the best technology to reproduce historical work in the same manner it was first published to preserve its original nature. Any marks or number seen are left intentionally to preserve its true form.

THE PREFACE.

THE *Discourse which I now offer to the Publick was drawn up on a very sorrowful Occasion; the Death of a most desirable Child, who was formed in such a Correspondence to my own Relish and Temper, as to be able to give me a Degree of Delight, and consequently of Distress, which I did not before think it possible I could have received from a little Creature who had not quite compleated her Fifth Year.*

Since the Sermon was preached, it has pleased GOD *to make the like Breaches on the Families of several of my Friends; and, with Regard to some of them, the Affliction hath been attended with Circumstances of yet sorer Aggravation. Tho' several of them are removed to a considerable Distance from me, and from each other I have born their Afflictions upon my Heart with cordial Sympathy; and it is with a particular Desire of serving them, that I have undertaken the sad Task of reviewing and transcribing these Papers; which may almost be called the Minutes of my own Sighs and Tears, over the poor Remains of my eldest and (of this Kind) dearest Hope, when they were not as yet* buried out of my Sight.

They are, indeed, full of Affection, and to be sure some may think they are too full of it: But let them consider the Subject, and the Circumstances, and surely they will pardon it. I apprehend, I could not have treated such a Subject coldly, had I writ upon it many years ago, when I was untaught in the School of Affliction, and knew nothing of such a Calamity as this, but by Speculation or Report: How much less could I do it, when GOD *had touched me in so tender a Part, and (to allude to a celebrated ancient Story,) called me out to appear on a publick Stage, as with an Urn in my Hand, which contained the Ashes of my own Child!*

In such a sad Situation Parents, at least, will forgive the Tears of a Parent, and those Meltings of Soul which overflow in the following Pages. I have not attempted to run thro' the Common place of immoderate Grief, *but have only selected a few obvious Thoughts which I found peculiarly suitable to myself; and, I bless* GOD, *I can truly say, they gave me a solid and substantial Relief, under a Shock of Sorrow, which would otherwise have broken my Spirits.*

On my own Experience, therefore, I would recommend them to others, in the like Condition, And let me intreat my Friends and Fellow-Sufferers to remember, that it is not a low Degree of Submission to the Divine Will, which is called for in the ensuing Discourse. It is comparatively an easy Thing to behave with external Decency, to refrain from bold Censures and outragious Complaints, or to speak in the outward Language of Resignation. But it is not, so easy to get rid of every repining Thought, and to forbear taking it, in some Degree at least, unkindly, that the GOD *whom we love and serve, in whose Friendship we have long trusted and rejoiced, should act what, to Sense, seems so unfriendly a Part: That he should take away a Child; and if a Child,* that Child; *and if that Child, at that Age; and if at that Age, with this or that particular Circumstance, which seems the very Contrivance of Providence to add double Anguish to the Wound; and all this, when he could so easily have recalled it; when we know him to have done it for so many others; when we so earnestly desired it; when we sought it with such Importunity, and yet, as we imagine, with so much Submission too:—That, notwithstanding all this; he should tear it away with an inexorable Hand, and leave us, it may be for a while, under the Load, without any extraordinary Comforts and Supports, to balance so grievous a Tryal.—In these Circumstances, not only to justify, but to glorify* GOD *in all,—chearfully to subscribe to his Will,—cordially to approve it as merciful and gracious,—so as to be able to say, as the pious and excellent Archbishop of* Cambray *did, when his Royal Pupil, and the Hopes of a Nation were taken away*‡ *, "If there needed no more than to move a Straw to bring him to Life again, I would not do it, since the Divine Pleasure is otherwise".—This, this is a difficult Lesson indeed; a Triumph of Christian Faith and Love, which I fear many of us are yet to learn.*

But let us follow after it, and watch against the first Rising of a contrary Temper, as most injurious to GOD, *and prejudicial to ourselves. To preserve us against it, let us review the Considerations now to be proposed, as what we are to digest into our Hearts, and work into our Thoughts and our Passions. And I would hope, that if we do in good earnest make the Attempt, we shall find this Discourse a cooling and sweetening Medicine, which may allay that inward Heat and Sharpness, with which, in a Case like ours, the Heart is often inflamed and corroded. I commend it, such as it is, to the Blessing of the great Physician, and could wish the Reader to make up its many Deficiencies, by Mr.* Flavel's Token for Mourners, *and Dr.* Grosvenor's Mourner; *to which, if it suit his Relish, he may please to add Sir* William Temple's Essay on the Excess of Grief: *Three Tracts which, in their very different Strains and Styles, I cannot but look upon as in the Number of the best which our Language, or, perhaps, any other, has produced upon this Subject.*

> *As for this little Piece of mine, I question not, but, like the Generality of single Sermons, it will soon be worn out and forgot. But in the mean time, I would humbly hope, that some tender Parent, whom Providence has joined with me in sad Similitude of Grief, may find some Consolation from it, while sitting by the Coffin of a beloved Child, or mourning over its Grave. And I particularly hope it, with Regard to those dear and valuable Friends, whose Sorrows, on the like Occasion, have lately been added to my own.*

I desire that, tho' they be not expressly named, they would please to consider this Sermon as most affectionately and respectfully dedicated to them; *and would, in Return, give me a Share in their Prayers, that all the Vicissitudes of Life may concur to quicken me in the Duties of it, and to ripen me for that blessed World, where I hope many of those dear Delights, which are now withering around us, will spring up in fairer and more durable Forms.* Amen.

Northampton,

Jan. 31, 1736-7.

POSTSCRIPT.

I could easily shew, with how much Propriety I have called the dear Deceased an amiable and hopeful Child, *by a great many little Stories, which Parents would perhaps read with Pleasure, and Children might hear with some Improvement: Yet as I cannot be sure that no others may happen to read the Discourse, I dare not trust my Pen and my Heart, on so delicate a Subject. One Circumstance I will however venture to mention, (as I see here is a Blank Page left,) which may indeed be consider'd as a Specimen of many others. As she was a great Darling with most of our Friends that knew her, she often received Invitations to different Places at the same Time; and when I once asked her, on such an Occasion, what made every Body love her so well; she answer'd me, (with that Simplicity and Spirit, which alas! Charm'd me too much,)* Indeed, Pappa, I cannot think, unless it be because I love every Body. *A Sentiment obvious to the Understanding of a Child, yet not unworthy the Reflection of the wisest Man*[*].

2 KINGS IV. 25, 26.

And it came to pass when the Man of GOD saw her afar off, that he said to Gehazi his Servant, Behold, yonder is that Shunamite: Run now, I pray thee, to meet her, and say unto her, Is it well with thee? Is it well with thine Husband? Is it well with the Child? And she answered, IT IS WELL.

WHEN the Apostle would encourage our Hope and Trust in the Tenderness of Christ as the great High Priest and convince us that he is capable of being touched with a sympathetick Sense of our Infirmities, he argues at large from this Consideration, that Jesus *was in all Points tempted like us;* so that as *he himself has suffer'd, being tempted, he knows how* more compassionately *to succour* those that are under the like Trials[a]. Now this must surely intimate, that it is not in human Nature, even in its most perfect State, so tenderly to commiserate any Sorrows, as those which our own Hearts have felt: As we cannot form a perfect Idea of any bitter Kind of Draught, by the most exact Description, till we have ourselves tasted it. It is probably for this Reason, amongst others, that GOD frequently exercises such, as have the Honour to be inferior Shepherds in the Flock of Christ, with a long Train of various Afflictions, *that we may be able to comfort them who are in* the like *Trouble, with those Consolations with which we have ourselves been comforted of GOD*[b]. And, if we have the Temper which becomes our Office, it will greatly reconcile us to our Trials, to consider, that from our weeping Eyes, and our bleeding Hearts, a Balm may be extracted to heal the Sorrows of others, and a Cordial to revive their fainting Spirits. May we never be left to sink under our Burden, in such a manner, that there should be room, after all that we have boasted of the Strength of religious Supports, to apply to us the Words of *Eliphaz* to *Job*[c], *Thou hast strengthen'd the weak Hands, and upheld him that was ready to fall; but now it is come upon thee, and thou faintest; it touches thee, and thou art troubled!* May we never behave, as if *the Consolations of GOD were small*[d]; lest it should be *as when a Standard-Bearer fainteth*[e], and whole Companies of Soldiers are thrown into Confusion and Distress!

MY Friends, you are Witnesses for me, that I have not stood by as an unconcerned Spectator amidst the Desolations of your respective Families, when GOD's awful Hand hath been lopping off those tender Branches from them, which were once our common Hope and Delight. I have often put my Soul in the stead of yours, and endeavour'd to give such a Turn to my publick as well as my private

Discourses, as might be a means of composing and chearing your Minds, and forming you to a submissive Temper, that you might *be subject to the Father of Spirits, and live*. In this View I have, at different Times, largely insisted on the Example of *Aaron, who held his peace*, when his two eldest Sons were struck dead in a Moment by Fire from the Lord, which destroyed them in the very Act of their Sin; and I have also represented that of *Job,* who, when the Death of ten Children by one Blow was added to the Spoil of his great Possessions, could say, *The Lord gave, and the Lord hath taken away; blessed be the Name of the Lord*. The Instance which is here before us, is not indeed so memorable as these; but to present Circumstances it is, in many Respects, more suitable: And it may the rather deserve our Notice, as it shews us the Wisdom, Composure, and Piety of one of the weaker and tenderer Sex, on an Occasion of such aggravated Distress, that had *Aaron* or *Job* behaved just as she did, we must have acknowledged, that they had not sunk beneath the Dignity of their Character, nor appear'd unworthy of our Applause, and our Imitation.

INDEED there may be some Reason to imagine, that it was with Design to humble those who are in distinguish'd Stations of Life, and who have peculiar Advantages and Obligations to excel in Religion, that GOD has shewn us in Scripture, as well as in common Life, some bright Examples of Piety, where they could hardly have been expected in so great a Degree; and hath, as it were, *perfected Praise out of the Mouths of Babes and Sucklings*. Thus when *Zacharias*, an aged Priest, doubted the Veracity of the Angel which appeared to assure him of the Birth of his Child, which was to be produced in an ordinary Way; *Mary,* an obscure young Virgin, could believe a far more unexampled Event, and said, with humble Faith and thankful Consent, *Behold the Hand-maid of the Lord, be it unto me according to thy Word*. *Jonah* the Prophet, tho' favour'd with such immediate Revelations, and so lately delivered, in a miraculous Way, from the very *Belly of Hell*, was thrown into a most indecent Transport of Passion, on the withering of a Gourd; so that he presumed to tell the Almighty to his Face, that *he did well to be angry even unto Death*: Whereas this pious Woman preserves the Calmness and Serenity of her Temper, when she had lost a Child, a Son, an only Child, who had been given beyond all natural Hope, and therefore to be sure was so much the dearer, and the Expectation from him so much the higher. Yet are these Expectations dash'd almost in a Moment; and this, when he was grown up to an Age when Children are peculiarly entertaining; for he was old enough to be with his Father in the Field, where no doubt he was diverting him with his fond Prattle; yet he was not too big to be laid *on his Mother's Knees*, when he came home complaining of his

Head; so that he was probably about five or six Years old. This amiable Child was well in the Morning, and dead by Noon; a pale Corpse in his Mother's Arms! and he now *lay dead in the House*; and yet they had the Faith, and the Goodness to say, "*It is well.*"

THIS good Woman had found the Prophet *Elisha* grateful for all the Favours he had received at her House; where she had from time to time accommodated him in his Journies, and thought it an Honour rather than an Incumbrance. She had experienced the Power of his Prayers, in answer to which the Child had been given; and 'tis extremely probable, that she also recollected the Miracle which *Elijah* had wrought a few Years before, tho' till that Time the like had not been known in *Israel*, or on Earth; I mean, in raising from the Dead the Child of that Widow of *Sarepta* , who had nourished him during the Famine. She might therefore think it a possible Case, that the Miracle might be renewed; at least, she knew not how to comfort herself better, than by going to so good a Friend, and asking his Counsels and his Prayers, to enable her to bear her Affliction, if it must not be removed ,

ACCORDINGLY she hasted to him; and he, on the other side, discovered the Temper of a real Friend, in the Message with which he sent *Gehazi* his Servant to meet her, *while she was yet afar off.* The Moment she appeared, the Concerns of her whole Family seem to have come into his kind Heart at once, and he particularly asks, *Is it well with thee? Is it well with thine Husband? Is it well with the Child?* A beautiful Example of that affectionate Care for the Persons and Families of their Friends, which Christian Ministers (who, like the Prophets of old, are called *Men of GOD*) should habitually bear about in their Hearts; which should be awakened by every Sight of them, and expressed on every proper Occasion.

HER Answer was very remarkable: *She said, It is well.* Perhaps she meant this, to divert the more particular Enquiry of the Servant; as she had before made the same Answer to her Husband, when he had examined into the Reason of her intended Journey, as probably not knowing of the sad Breach which had been made: *She said, It is well* ; which was a civil way of intimating her Desire that he would not ask any more particular Questions. But I cannot see any Reason to restrain the Words to this Meaning alone: We have ground to believe, from the Piety she expressed in her first Regards to *Elisha,* and the Opportunities which she had of improving in Religion by the frequent Converse of that holy Man, that when she used this Language, she intended thereby to express her Resignation to the Divine Will in what had lately pass'd: And this might be the Meaning of her Heart, (tho' one ignorant of the Particulars of her Case, might not fully understand it from such ambiguous Words;) "*It is well* on the whole. Though my Family be afflicted, we are afflicted in Faithfulness; tho' my dear Babe be dead, yet my Heavenly Father is just, and he is good in all. He knows how to bring Glory to himself, and Advantage to us, from this Stroke. Whether this Application do, or do not succeed, whether the Child be, or be not restored, *it is* still *well*; *well* with him, and *well* with us; for we are in such wise and such gracious Hands, that I would not allow one murmuring Word, or one repining Thought." So that, on the whole, the Sentiment of this good *Shunamite* was much the same with that of *Hezekiah*, when he answered to that dreadful Threatning which imported the Destruction of his Children, *Good is the Word of the Lord which he hath spoken*; or that of *Job*, when he heard that all his Sons and his Daughters were crushed under the Ruins of their elder Brother's House, and yet (in the fore-cited Words) *blessed the Name of the Lord.*

Now this is the Temper to which, by divine Assistance, we should all labour to bring our own Hearts, when GOD puts this bitter Cup into our Hands, and *takes away with a Stroke* those dear Little-ones, which were the *Desire of our Eyes*, and the Joy of our Hearts. Let us not content ourselves, in such Circumstances, with *keeping the Door of our Lips*, that we break not out into any Indecencies of Complaint; let us not attempt to harden ourselves against our Sorrows by a stern Insensibility, or that sullen Resolution which sometimes says, *It is a Grief, and I must bear it* ; but let us labour, (for *a great Labour* it will indeed be,) to compose and quiet our Souls, calmly to acquiesce in this painful Dispensation, nay, cordially to approve it as in present Circumstances every Way fit.

IT will be the main Business of this Discourse, to prove how reasonable such a Temper is, or to shew how much Cause Christian Parents have to borrow the Language of the Text, when their Infant Offspring is taken away, and to say with the pious *Shunamite*, in the noblest Sense that her Words will bear,—*It is well.*

AND here I would more particularly shew,—It is well in the general, because GOD does it:—It is surely well for the pious Parents in particular, because it is the Work of their Covenant GOD:—They may see many Respects in which it is evidently so, by observing what useful Lessons it has a Tendency to teach them:—And they have Reason to hope, it is well with those dear Creatures whom GOD hath removed in their early Days.

THESE are surely convincing Reasons to the Understanding: Yet who can say, that they shalt be Reasons to the Heart? *Arise, O GOD, and plead thine own Cause*, in the most effectual Manner! May thy powerful and gracious Voice appease the swelling Billows of the Passions, and produce a great and delightful Calm in our Souls, in which we may yet enjoy thee and ourselves, tho' a Part of our Treasure be for the present swallowed up!

I. THERE is surely Reason, in such a Case, to say *it is well*,—because GOD doth it.

THIS pass'd for an unanswerable Reason with *David, I was dumb, I opened not my Mouth, because thou didst it*, and with good old *Eli*, under a severer Tryal than ours, *It is the Lord, let him do as seemeth good in his Sight*. And shall We object against the Force of it? Was it a Reason to *David*, and to *Eli*, and is it not equally so to us? Or have We any new Right to *reply against GOD*, which those eminent Saints had not?

His kingdom ruleth over all; and there is *not* so much as *a Sparrow that falls to the Ground without our Father, but the very Hairs of our Head are all number'd* by him. Can we then imagine that our dear Children fall into their Graves without his Notice or Interposition? Did that watchful Eye that *keepeth Israel*, now, for the first time, *slumber and sleep*, and an Enemy lay hold on that fatal Moment to bear away these precious Spoils, and bury our Joys and our Hopes in the Dust? Did some malignant Hand stop up the Avenues of Life, and break its Springs, so as to baffle all the Tenderness of the Parent, and all the Skill of the Physician? Whence does such a Thought come, and whither would it lead? Diseases and Accidents are but second Causes, which owe all their Operations to the continued Energy of the great original Cause. Therefore GOD says, *I will bereave them of Children*; *I take away the Desire of thine Eyes with a Stroke*. *He changeth their Countenance, and sendeth them away*. *Thou Lord turnest Man to Destruction, and sayest, Return ye Children of Men* . And what shall we say? Are not the Administrations of his Providence wise and good? Can we *teach him Knowledge*? Can we tax him with Injustice? Shall the Most High GOD learn of us how to govern the World, and be instructed by our Wisdom when to remove his Creatures from one State of Being to another? Or do we imagine that his Administration, in the general Right and Good, varies when he comes to *touch our Bone and our Flesh* ? Is that the secret Language of our Soul, "That *it is well*, others should drink of the Cup, but not We; that any Families but ours should be broken, and any Hearts but ours should be wounded?" Who might not claim the like Exemption? and what would become of the Divine Government in general; or where would be his obedient Homage from his Creatures, if each should begin to complain, as soon as it comes to his own Turn to suffer? Much fitter is it for us to conclude, that our own Afflictions may be as reasonable as those of others; that amidst all the *Clouds and Darkness* of this present Dispensation, *Righteousness and Judgment are the Habitation of his Throne* ; and, in a word, that *it is well*, because GOD hath done it. It suits the general Scheme of the Divine Providence, and to an obedient submissive Creature that might be enough; but it is far from being all. For,

II. PIOUS PARENTS, under such a Dispensation, may conclude *it is well for them* in particular,—because he, who hath done it, is their Covenant GOD.

THIS is the great Promise, to which all the Saints under the Old and New Testament are Heirs, *I will be to them a God, and they shall be to me a People*[m] : And if we are interested in it, the happy Consequence is, that we being his, all our Concerns are his also; all are humbly resigned to him,—and graciously administer'd by him,—and incomparably better Blessings bestowed and secured, than any which the most afflictive Providence can remove.

IF we have any Share in this everlasting Covenant, all that we are or have, must, of course, have been *solemnly surrender'd* to GOD. And this is a Thought peculiarly applicable to the Case immediately in view. "Did I not," may the Christian, in such a sad Circumstance, generally say, "did I not, in a very solemn Manner, bring this my Child to God in Baptism, and in that Ordinance recognize his Right to it? Did I not, with all humble *Subjection to the Father of Spirits*[n] , and *Father of Mercies*[o], lay it down at his Feet, perhaps with an express, at least to be sure with a tacit Consent, that it should be disposed of by him, as his infinite Wisdom and Goodness should direct, whether for Life or for Death? And am I now to complain of him, because he has removed not only a Creature of his own, but one of the Children of his Family? Or shall I pretend, after all, to set up a Claim in Opposition to his? A Heathen Parent, even from the Light of Nature, might have learn'd silent Submission: How much more then a Christian Parent, who hath presented his Child to GOD in this initiatory Ordinance; and perhaps also many a time, both before and since, hath presented himself at the Table of the Lord! Have I not there taken that *Cup of Blessings*, with a declared Resolution of accepting every other *Cup* how bitter soever it might be, *which my heavenly Father* should see fit to *put into my Hand*[p]? When I have perhaps felt some painful Fore-bodings of what I am now suffering; I have, in my own Thoughts, particularly singled out that dear Object of my Cares and my Hopes, to lay it down anew at my Father's Feet, and say, *Lord thou gavest it to me, and I resign it to thee;*

continue, or remove it, as thou pleasest. And did I then mean to trifle with GOD? Did I mean in effect to say, *Lord, I will give it up, if thou wilt not take it?"*

REFLECT farther, I beseech you, on your *secret Retirements*, and think, as surely some of you may, "How often have I there been on my Knees before GOD on account of this Child; and what was then my Language? Did I say, Lord, I absolutely insist on its Recovery; I cannot, on any Terms or any Considerations whatsoever, bear to think of losing it?" Sure we were none of us so indecently transported with the fondest Passion, as to be so *rash with our Mouths* as *to utter such Things before* the Great GOD[q]. Such Presumption had deserv'd a much heavier Punishment than we are now bearing, and, if not retracted, may perhaps still have it.—Did not one or another of us rather say, "Lord, I would humbly intreat, with all due Submission to thy superior Wisdom and sovereign Pleasure, that my Child may live; but if it must be otherwise, *not my Will, but thine be done*[e] ? I and mine are in thine Hand, *do with me*, and with them, *as seemeth good in thy Sight*[s] ". And do we now blame ourselves for this? Would we unsay it again, and, if possible, take ourselves and our Children out of his Hands, whom we have so often owned as all-wise and all-gracious, and have chosen as our great Guardian and theirs?

LET it farther be consider'd, it is done by that GOD who has *accepted of this Surrender*, so as to undertake the Administration of our Affairs: "He is become my Covenant GOD in Christ," may the Christian say; "and, in consequence of that Covenant, he hath engaged to manage the Concerns and Interests of his People so, that *all Things shall work together for good to them that love him*[t] : And do I not love him? Answer, Oh my Heart, dost thou not love thy GOD much better than all the Blessings which Earth can boast, or which the Grave hath swallowed up? Wouldst thou resign thine Interest in him to recover these precious Spoils, to receive this dear Child from the Dust, a thousand times fairer and sweeter than before? Rather let Death devour every remaining Comfort, and leave me alone with him; with whom when I indeed am, I miss not the Creatures, but rather rejoice in their Absence, as I am then more intire with *him whom my Soul loveth*. And if I do indeed love him, this Promise is mine, and *all Things*, and therefore this sad Event in particular, *shall work together for my good*. Shall I not then say, *It is well?* What if it exceeded all the Stretch of my Thoughts, to conceive *how* it could, in any Instance, be so? What are my narrow Conceptions, that they should pretend to circumscribe infinite Wisdom, Faithfulness, and Mercy? Let me rather, with *Abraham, give Glory to God, and in Hope believe against Hope*[u] ".

ONCE more; let us consider how many *invaluable Blessings* are given us by this Covenant, and then judge whether we have not the utmost Reason to acquiesce in such an Event of Providence. "If I am in Covenant with God," may the Believer say, "then he hath pardoned my Sins, and renewed my Heart, and hath made his blessed Spirit dwelling in me, the sacred Bond of an everlasting Union between him and my Soul. He is leading me through the Wilderness, and will, ere long, lead me out of it to the heavenly *Canaan*. And how far am I already arrived in my Journey thither, now that I am come to the Age of losing a Child! And when GOD hath done all this for me, is he rashly to be suspected of Unkindness? *He that spared not his own Son*[v], he that gave me with him his Spirit and his Kingdom, why doth he deny, or why doth he remove, any other Favour? Did he think the Life of this Child too great a Good to grant, when he thought not Christ and Glory too precious? Away with that Thought, Oh my unbelieving Heart, and with every Thought which would derogate from such rich amazing Grace, or would bring any thing in comparison with it. Art thou under these Obligations to him, and wilt thou yet complain? With what Grace, with what Decency canst thou dispute this, or any other Matter, with thy GOD? *What Right have I yet to cry any more to the King?*[x] " Would any of you, my Brethren, venture to say, "What tho' I be a Child of GOD, and an Heir of Glory, it matters not, for *my Gourd is withered*; that pleasant Plant which was opening so fair and so delightful, under the Shadow of which I expected long to have sate, and even *the Rock of Ages* cannot shelter me so well? I can behold that beloved Face no more, and therefore I will not look upward to behold the Face of GOD, I will not look forward to Christ and to Heaven?" Would this, my Friends, be the Language of a real Christian? Nay, are there not many abandon'd Sinners who would tremble at such Expressions? Yet is it not in effect the Language of our tumultuous Passions, when, like *Rachel,* we are *mourning for our Children,* and *will not be comforted, because they are not*[y]? Is it not our Language while we cannot, like the pious *Shunamite* in the Text, bring our afflicted Hearts to say, *It is well?*

III. PIOUS PARENTS, in such a Circumstance, have farther Reason to say, *It is well,*—as they may observe an apparent Tendency in such a Dispensation to teach them a Variety of the most instructive and useful Lessons, in a very convincing and effectual Manner.

'TIS a just Observation of *Solomon,* that *the Rod and Reproof give Wisdom*[z] ; and 'tis peculiarly applicable to such a Chastisement of our heavenly Father. It should therefore be our great Care to *bear the Rod and him that hath appointed it*[a] ; and so far as it hath a Tendency to teach us our

Duty, and to improve the divine Life in our Souls, we have the highest Reason to say, that *it is* indeed *well.*

EVERY Affliction hath in its Degree this kind of Tendency, and 'tis the very Reason for which *we are* thus *chastened,* that we may *profit* by our Sorrows, and be made *Partakers of God's Holiness*[b]. But this Dispensation is peculiarly adapted, in a very affecting Manner,—to teach us the Vanity of the World,—to warn us of the Approach of our own Death,—to quicken us in the Duties incumbent upon us, especially to our surviving Children,—and to produce a more intire Resignation to the Divine Will, which is indeed the surest Foundation of Quiet, and Source of Happiness.

SHALL insist a little more particularly on each of these; and I desire that it may be remembered, that the Sight and Knowledge of such mournful Providences as are now before us, should, in some Degree, be improved to these Purposes, even by those Parents whose Families are most prosperous and joyful: May they learn Wisdom and Piety from what *we* suffer, and their Improvements shall be acknowledged as an additional Reason for *us* to say, *It is well.*

1. WHEN GOD takes away our Children from us, it is a very affecting Lesson of the Vanity of the World.

THERE is hardly a Child born into it, on whom the Parents do not look with some pleasing Expectation that it shall *comfort them concerning their Labour*[c] . This makes the Toil of Education easy and delightful: And truly 'tis very early that we begin to find a Sweetness in it, which abundantly repays all the Fatigue. Five, or four, or three, or two Years, make Discoveries which afford immediate Pleasure, and which suggest future Hopes. Their Words, their Actions, their very Looks touch us, if they be amiable and promising Children, in a tender, but very powerful Manner; their little Arms twine about our Hearts; and there is something more penetrating in their first broken Accents of Indearment, than in all the Pomp and Ornament of Words. Every Infant-Year increases the Pleasure, and nourishes the Hope. And where is the Parent so wise and so cautious, and so constantly intent on his Journey to Heaven, as not to measure back a few Steps to Earth again, on such a plausible and decent Occasion, as that of introducing the young Stranger into the Amusements, nay perhaps, where Circumstances will admit it, into the Elegancies of Life, as well as its more serious and important Business? What fond Calculations do we form of what it *will be,* from what *it is*! How do we in Thought open every Blossom of Sprightliness, or Humanity, or Piety, to its full Spread, and ripen it to a sudden Maturity! But, oh, who shall teach those that have never felt it, how it tears the very Soul; when GOD roots up the tender Plant with an inexorable Hand, and withers the Bud in which the Colours were beginning to glow! Where is now our Delight? Where is our Hope? Is it in the Coffin? Is it in the Grave? Alas! all the Loveliness of Person, of Genius, and of Temper, serves but to point and to poison the Arrow, which is drawn out of our own Quiver to wound us. Vain, delusive, transitory Joys! "And such, Oh my Soul," will the Christian say, "such are thine earthly Comforts in every Child, in every Relative, in every Possession of Life; such are the Objects of thy Hopes, and thy Fears, thy Schemes, and thy Labours, where Earth alone is concerned. Let me then, once for all, direct mine Eyes to another and a better State. From these *broken Cisterns*, the Fragments of which may hurt me indeed, but can no longer refresh me, let me look to the *Fountain of living Waters*[f]. From these setting, Stars, or rather these bright but vanishing Meteors, which make my Darkness so much the more sensible, let me turn to the *Father of Lights*. Oh Lord, *What wait I for? my Hope is in thee*[g], my Pure Abode, my everlasting Confidence! My Gourds wither, my Children die; but *the Lord liveth, and blessed be my Rock, and let the God of my Salvation be exalted*. I see, in one Instance more, the sad Effects of having over-loved the Creature; let me endeavour for the future, by the Divine Assistance, to fix my Affections there where they cannot exceed; but where all the Ardor of them will be as much my Security and my Happiness, as it is now my Snare and my Distress."

2. THE Removal of our Children by such awful Strokes may warn us of the Approach of our own Death.

HEREBY GOD doth very sensibly shew us, and those around us, that *all Flesh is as Grass, and all the Glory* and Loveliness *of it like the Flower of the Field*. And when our own Habitations are made the Houses of Mourning, and ourselves the Leaders in that sad Procession, it may surely be expected that we should lay it to Heart, so as to be quicken'd and improved by the View. "Have my Children died in the Morning of their Days, and can I promise myself that I shall see the Evening of mine? Now perhaps may I say, in a more literal Sense than ever, *The Graves are ready for me*[h]. One of my Family, and some of us may add, the First-born of it, is gone as it were to take Possession of the Sepulchre in all our Names; and ere long I shall lie down with my Child in the same Bed; yea perhaps many of the Feet that followed it shall attend me thither. Our Dust shortly shall be blended together; and who can tell but this Providence might chiefly be intended as a Warning Blow to me, that these concluding Days of my Life might be more regular, more spiritual, more useful than the former?"

3. THE Providence before us may be farther improved to quicken us in the Duties of Life, and especially in the Education of surviving Children.

IT is, on the Principles I hinted above, an Engagement, that *whatever our Hand findeth to do, we should do it with all our Might,* since it so plainly shews us that we are *going to the Grave, where there is no Device, nor Knowledge, nor Working*: But permit me especially to observe, how peculiarly the Sentiments we feel on these sad Occasions, may be improved for the Advantage of our dear Offspring who yet remain, and quicken us to a proper Care in their religious Education.

We all see that it is a very reasonable Duty, and every Christian Parent resolves that he will *ere long* apply himself to it; but I am afraid, great Advantages are lost by a Delay, which we think we can easily excuse. Our Hands are full of a Variety of Affairs, and our Children are yet very young: We are therefore ready to imagine 'tis a good Husbandry of Time to defer our Attempts for their Instruction to a more *convenient Season*[k] , when they may be able to learn more in an Hour, than the Labour of Days could now teach them; besides that we are apprehensive of Danger in over-loading their tender Spirits, especially when they are perhaps under Indisposition, and need to be diverted, rather than gravely advised and instructed.

BUT I beseech you, my Friends, let us view the Matter with that Impartiality, which the Eloquence of Death hath a Tendency to produce. "That lovely Creature that GOD hath now taken away, tho' its Days were few, tho' its Faculties were weak, yet might it not have known a great deal more of Religion than it did, and felt a great deal more of it too, had I faithfully and prudently done my Part? How did it learn Language so soon, and in such a Compass and Readiness? Not by multiplied Rules, nor labour'd Instruction, but by Conversation. And might it not have learn'd much more of Divine Things by Conversation too, if they had been allowed a due Share in our Thoughts and our Discourses; according to the Charge given to the *Israelites,* to *talk of them going out and coming in, lying down and rising up*[l] ? How soon did it learn Trifles, and retain them, and after its little way observe and reason upon them, perhaps with a Vivacity that sometimes surprized me! And had I been as diligent as I ought, who can tell what Progress it might have made in Divine Knowledge? Who can tell but, as a Reward to these pious Cares, GOD might have put a Word into its dying Lips, which I might all my Life have recollected with Pleasure, and *out of its* feeble *Mouth might have perfected Praise*[m]?"

My Friends, let us humble ourselves deeply before GOD under a Sense of our past Neglects, and let us learn our future Duty. We may perhaps be ready fondly to say, "Oh that it were possible my Child could be restored to me again, tho' it were but for a few Weeks or Days! how diligently would I attempt to supply my former Deficiencies!" Unprofitable Wish! Yet may the Thought be improved for the good of surviving Children. How shall we express our Affection to them? Not surely by indulging all the Demands of Appetite and Fancy, in many early Instances so hazardous, and so fatal; not by a Solicitude to treasure up Wealth for them, whose only Portion may perhaps be a little Coffin and Shrowd. No; our truest Kindness to them will be to endeavour, by Divine Grace, to form them to an early Inquiry after GOD, and Christ, and Heaven, and a Love for real Goodness in all the Forms of it which may come within their Observation and Notice. Let us apply ourselves immediately to this Talk, as those that remember there is a double Uncertainty, in their Lives, and in ours. In a Word, let us be *that* with regard to every Child that yet remains, which we proposed and engaged to be to that which is taken away, when we pleaded with GOD for the Continuance of its Life, at least for a little while, that it might be farther assisted in the Preparations for Death and Eternity. If such Resolutions be formed and pursued, the Death of one may be the Means of spiritual Life to many; and we shall surely have Reason to say *it is well*, if it teach us so useful a Lesson.

4. THE Providence before us may have a special Tendency to improve our Resignation to the Divine Will; and if it does so, it will indeed be *well*.

THERE is surely no imaginable Situation of Mind so sweet and so reasonable, as that which we feel, when we humbly refer ourselves in all Things to the Divine Disposal, in an intire Suspension of our own Will, seeing and owning the Hand of GOD, and bowing before it with a filial Acquiescence. This is chiefly to be learn'd from suffering; and perhaps there is no Suffering which is fitter to teach it, than this. In many other Afflictions there is such a Mixture of human Interposition, that we are ready to imagine, we may be allowed to complain, and to chide a little. Indignation mingles itself with our Grief; and when it does so, it warms the Mind, tho' with a feverish Kind of Heat, and in an unnatural Flow of Spirits, leads the Heart into a Forgetfulness of GOD. But here it is so apparently his Hand, that we must refer it to him, and it will appear bold Impiety to quarrel at what is done. In other Instances we can at least flatter ourselves with Hope, that the Calamity may be diverted, or the Enjoyment recovered; but here alas! there is no Hope. "Tears will not," as Sir *William Temple* finely expresses it, "water the lovely Plant so as to cause it to grow again; Sighs will not give it new Breath, nor can we furnish it with Life and Spirits by the Waste of our own." The Sentence is finally gone forth, and the last fatal Stroke irrecoverably given. Opposition is vain; a forced Submission gives but little Rest to the Mind; a cordial Acquiescence in the Divine Will is the only thing in the whole World that can ease the labouring Heart, and restore true Serenity. Remaining Corruption will work on such an Occasion, and a painful Struggle will convince the Christian how imperfect his present Attainments are: And this will probably lead him to an attentive Review of the great Reasons for Submission; it will lead him to urge them on his own Soul, and to plead them with GOD in Prayer; till at length the Storm is laid, and *Tribulation worketh Patience, and Patience Experience, and Experience a Hope which maketh not ashamed,* while *the Love of God is so shed abroad in the Heart*, as to humble it for every preceding Opposition, and to bring it even to a real Approbation of all that so wise and good a Friend hath done; resigning every other Interest and Enjoyment to his Disposal, and fitting do with the sweet Resolution of the Prophet, *Tho' the Fig-tree do not blossom, and there be no Fruit in the Vine, &c. yet will I rejoice in the Lord, and joy in the God of my Salvation.* And when we are brought to this, the whole Horizon clears, and the Sun breaks forth in its Strength.

NOW I appeal to every sincere Christian in the Assembly, whether there will not be Reason indeed to say *it is well*, if by this painful Affliction we more sensibly learn the Vanity of the Creature and we are awakened to serious Thoughts of our own latter End; if by it we are quickned in the Duties of Life, and formed to a more intire Resignation of Soul, and Acquiescence in the Divine Will. I shall only add once more, and 'tis a Thought of delightful Importance,

IV. THAT pious Parents have Reason to hope *it is well* with those dear Creatures who are taken away in their early Days.

I SEE not that the Word of GOD hath any whit passed a damnatory Sentence on any Infants; and it has not, I am sure we have no Authority to doubt, especially considering with how much Compassion the Divine Being speaks of them in the Instance of the *Ninevites*, and on some other Occasions. Perhaps, as some pious Divines have conjectured, they may constitute a very considerable Part of Number of the Elect, and, *as in Adam* they *all died,* they may *in Christ all be made alive*. At least, methinks, from the Covenant which GOD made with *Abraham*, and his Seed, *the Blessings of which* are *come upon the* believing *Gentiles*, there is Reason to hope well concerning the

Infant Offspring of GOD'S People, early devoted, and often recommended to him, that their *Souls* will be *bound in the Bundle of Life*, and *be loved for their Parents Sakes*.

IT is, indeed, impossible for us to say, how soon Children may be capable of contracting personal Guilt. They are quickly able to distinguish, some Degree, between Right and Wrong; and 'tis too plain, that they as quickly, in many Instances, forget the Distinction. The Corruptions of Nature begin early to work, and shew the Need of sanctifying Grace; yet, without a Miracle, it cannot be expected that much of the Christian Scheme should be understood by these little Creatures, in the first dawning of Reason, tho' a few evangelical Phrases may be taught, and, sometimes, by a happy kind of Accident, may be rightly applied. The tender Heart of a Parent may, perhaps, take a Hint, from hence to terrify itself, and exasperate all its other Sorrows, by that sad Thought, "What if my dear Child be perished for ever? gone from our Embraces, and all the little Pleasures we could give it, to everlasting Darkness and Pain?" Horrible Imagination! And Satan may, perhaps, take the Advantage of these gloomy Moments, to aggravate every little Infirmity into a Crime, and to throw us into an Agony, which no other View of the Affliction can possibly give, to a Soul penetrated with a Sense of Eternity. Nor do I know a Thought, in the whole Compass of Nature, that hath a more powerful Tendency to produce suspicious Notions of GOD, and a secret Alienation of Heart from him.

NOW for this very Reason, methinks, we should guard against so harsh a Conclusion, lest we, at once, injure the Divine Being, and torture ourselves. And, surely, we may easily fall on some Reflections which may incourage our Hopes, where *little Children* are concerned; and 'tis only of that Case that I am now speaking. Let us think of the blessed GOD, as the great Parent of universal Nature; whose *tender Mercies are over all his Works*; who declares that Judgment is *his strange Work*[u]; who *is very pitiful, and of tender Mercy*[w], *gracious and full of Compassion*[x]; who *delighteth in Mercy*[y]; who *waiteth to be gracious*[z]; and *endureth, with much Long-suffering, even the Vessels of Wrath fitted to Destruction*[a]. He intimately *knows our Frame*[b], and our Circumstances; he sees the Weakness of the unformed Mind; how forcibly the volatile Spirits are struck with a thousand new amusing Objects around it, and born away as a Feather before the Wind; and, on the other hand, how, when Distempers seize it, the feeble Powers are over-born in a Moment, and render'd incapable of any Degree of Application and Attention. And, Lord, wilt thou *open thine Eyes on such a one, to bring it into* strict *Judgment with thee* ? Amidst all the Instances of thy Patience, and thy Bounty, to the most abandon'd of Mankind, are these little helpless Creatures the Objects of thy speedy Vengeance, and final Severity?

LET us farther consider, as it is a very comfortable Thought in these Circumstances, the compassionate Regard which the blessed *Jesus* expressed to little Children. He was *much displeased* with those who forbad their being *brought* to him; *and said, Suffer them to come unto me, and forbid them not, for of such is the Kingdom of* GOD; and *taking them up in his Arms, he laid his Hands upon them, and blessed them*. In another Instance we are told, that he *took a little Child,* (who appears to have been old enough to come at his Call,) and *set him in the Midst of his Disciples, and said, Except ye become as little Children, you shall in no wise enter into the kingdom of Heaven*. May we not then hope that many little Children are admitted into it? And may not that Hope be greatly confirmed from whatever, of an amiable and regular Disposition, we have observed in those that are taken away? If we have seen *a Tenderness of Conscience in any thing which they apprehended would displease the great and good* GOD*; a Love to Truth; a Readiness to attend on Divine Worship, from some imperfect Notion of its general Design, though the Particulars of it could not be understood; an open, candid, benevolent Heart; a tender Sense of Obligation, and a Desire, according to their little Power, to repay it*; may we not hope that these were some of the *first Fruits of the Spirit*, which he would, in due Time, have ripened into Christian Graces, and are now, on a sudden, perfected by that great Almighty Agent *who worketh all, and in all* ?

SURE I am, that this blessed Spirit hath no inconsiderable Work to perform on the most established Christians, to finish them to a complete Meetness for the Heavenly World: Would to GOD, there were no greater Blemishes to be observed in their Character, than the little Vanities of Children! With infinite Ease then can he perfect what is lacking in their unfinished Minds, and pour out upon them, in a Moment, that Light and Grace, which shall qualify them for a State, in Comparison of which, ours on Earth is but Childhood or Infancy.

NOW what a noble Source of Consolation is here! Then may the affectionate Parent say, "*It is well,* not only with me, but *with the Child* too: Incomparably better than if my ardent Wishes, and importunate Prayers for its Recovery, had been answered. *It is* indeed *well,* if that beloved Creature be *fallen asleep in Christ*; if that dear Lamb be folded in the Arms of the compassionate Shepherd, and gathered into his gracious Bosom. Self-love might have led me to wish its longer Continuance here; but if I truly *loved* my Child with a solid, rational Affection, I should much rather *rejoice,* to think *it is gone to* a heavenly

Father, and to the World of perfected Spirits above. Had it been spared to me, how slowly could I have taught it! and in the full Ripeness of its Age, what had it been, when compared with what it now is! How is it shot up on a sudden, from the Converse and the Toys of Children, to be a Companion with Saints and Angels, in the Employment, and the Blessedness of Heaven! Shall I then complain of it as a rigorous Severity to my Family, that GOD hath taken it to the Family above? And what if he hath chosen to bestow the distinguished Favour on *that one* of my little Flock, who was formed to take the tenderest Hold of my Heart? Was there Unkindness in that? What if he saw, that the very Sprightliness and Softness which made it to me so exquisitely delightful, might, in Time, have betrayed it into Ruin; and took this Method of sheltering it from Trials which had, otherwise, been too hard for it, and so fixing a Seal on its Character and Happiness? What if that strong Attachment of my Heart to it, had been a Snare to the Child, and to me? Or what if it had been otherwise? Do I need additional Reasons to justify the Divine Conduct, in an Instance which my Child is celebrating in the Songs of Heaven? If it is a new and untasted Affliction to have such a tender Branch lopp'd off, it is also a new Honour to be the Parent of a glorified Saint." And, as good Mr. *Howe* expressed it on another Occasion, "*If GOD be pleased, and his glorified Creature be pleased, who are we that we should be displeased?*"

"Could I wish, that this young Inhabitant of Heaven should be degraded to Earth again? Or would it thank me for that With? Would it say, that it was the Part of a wife Parent, to call it down from a Sphere of finch exalted Services and Pleasures, to our low Life here upon Earth? Let me rather be thankful for the pleasing Hope, that tho' GOD loves my Child too well to permit it to return to me, he will ere long bring me to it. And then that endeared paternal Affection, which would have been a Cord to tie me to Earth, and have added new Pangs to my Removal from it, will be asa golden Chain to draw me upwards, and add one farther Charm and Joy even to Paradise itself." And oh, how great a Joy to view the Change, and to compare that dear Idea, so fondly laid up, so often reviewed, with the now glorious Original, in the Improvements of the upper World! To borrow the Words of the sacred Writer, in a very different Sense? "*I said, I was desolate and bereaved of Children, and who hath brought up these? I was left alone, and these where have they been?* Was this my Desolation? this my Sorrow? to part with thee for a few Days, *that I might receive thee for Ever* , and find thee what thou now art!" It is for no Language, but that of Heaven, to describe the sacred Joy which such a Meeting must occasion.

IN the mean time, Christians, let us keep up the lively Expectation of it, and let what has befallen us draw our Thoughts upwards. Perhaps they will sometimes, before we are aware, sink to the Grave, and dwell in the Tombs that contain the poor Remains of what was once so dear to us. But let them take Flight from thence to more noble, more delightful Scenes. And I will add, let the Hope we have of the Happiness of our Children render GOD still dearer to our Souls. We feel a very tender Sense of the Kindness which our Friends expressed towards them, and think, indeed very justly, that their affectionate Care for them lays a lasting Obligation upon us. What Love then, and what Service do we owe to thee, oh gracious Father, who hast, we hope, received them into thine House above, and art now entertaining them there with unknown Delight, tho' our former Methods of Commerce with them be cut off! "Lord," should each of us say in such a Case, "I would take what thou art doing to my Child as done to my self, and as a Specimen and Earnest of what shall shortly be done." *It is* therefore *well*.

IT only remains, that I conclude with a few Hints of farther Improvement.

1. LET pious Parents, who have lost hopeful Children *in a maturer Age*, join with others in saying, *It is well*.

MY Friends, the Reasons which I have been urging at large, are common to you with us; and permit me to add, that as your Case has its peculiar Distress, it has, I think, in a yet greater Degree, its peculiar Consolations too.

I KNOW you will say, that it is inexpressibly grievous and painful, to part with Children who were grown up into most amiable Friends, who were your Companions in the Ways of GOD, and concerning whom you had a most agreeable Prospect, that they would have been the Ornaments and Supports of Religion in the rising Age, and extensive Blessings to the World, long after you had quitted it. These Reasonings have, undoubtedly, their Weight; and they have so, when considered in a very different View. Must you not acknowledge *it is well*, that you enjoyed so many Years of Comfort in them? that you reaped so much solid Satisfaction from them? and saw those Evidences of a Work of Grace upon their Hearts, which give you such abundant Reason to conclude that they are now received to that Inheritance of Glory, for which they were so apparently *made meet*? Some of them, perhaps, had already quitted their Father's House: As for others, had GOD spared their Lives, they might have been transplanted into Families of their own: And if, instead of being removed to another House, or Town, or County, they are taken by GOD into another World, is that a Matter of so great Complaint; when that World is so much better, and you are yourselves so near it? I put it to your Hearts, Christians, Would you rather have chosen to have buried them in their Infancy, or never to have known the Joys and the Hopes of a Parent, now you know the Vicissitude of Sorrow, and of Disappointment? But perhaps, you will say, that you chiefly grieve for that Loss which the World has sustained by the Removal of those, from whom it might reasonably have expected so much future Service. This is, indeed, a generous, and a Christian Sentiment, and there is something noble in those Tears which flow on such a Consideration. But do not so remember your Relation to Earth, as to forget that which you bear to Heaven; and do not so wrong the Divine Wisdom and Goodness, as to suppose, that when he takes away from hence promising Instruments of Service, he there lays them by as useless. Much more reasonable is it to conclude, that their Sphere of Action, as well as Happiness, is inlarged, and that the Church above hath gained incomparably more, than that below can be supposed to have lost by their Death.

ON the whole, therefore, far from complaining of the Divine Conduct in this Respect, it will become you, my Friends, rather to be very thankful that these dear Children were spared so long; to accompany and entertain you in so many Stages of your short Journey thro' Life, to answer so many of your Hopes, and to establish so many more beyond all Fear of Disappointment. Reflect on all that GOD did in, and upon them, on all he was beginning to do by them, and on what you have great Reason to believe he is now doing for them; and adore his Name, that he has left you these dear Memorials, by which your Case is so happily distinguished from ours, whose Hopes in our Children withered in the very Bud; or from theirs, who saw those who were once so dear to them, perishing, as they have Cause to fear, *in the Paths of the Destroyer.*

BUT while I speak thus, methinks I am alarmed, lest I should awaken the far more grievous Sorrows of some mournful Parent, whom it will not be so easy to comfort. My Brethren and Friends, what shall I say to you, who are lamenting over your *Absaloms*, and almost wishing *you had died for them*? Shall I urge *you* to say *it is well*? Perhaps you may think it a great Attainment, if, like *Aaron*, when his Sons *died before the Lord*, you *can hold your Peace*, under the awful Stroke. My Soul is troubled for you; *my Words are* almost *swallowed up*. I cannot unsay what I have elsewhere said at large on this melancholy Subject. Yet let me remind you of this, that you do not certainly know what Almighty

Grace might do for these lamented Creatures, even in the latest Moments, and have therefore no Warrant confidently to pronounce that they are assuredly perished. And if you cannot but tremble in the too probable Fear of it, labour to turn your Eyes from so dark a Prospect, to those better Hopes which GOD is setting before *you*. For surely you still have abundant Reason to rejoice in that Grace, which gives your own *Lives to you as a Prey*, and has brought you so near to that blessed World, where, hard as it is now to conceive it, you will have laid aside every Affection of Nature, which interferes with the Interests of GOD, and prevents your most chearful Acquiescence in every Particular of his wise and gracious Determinations.

2. FROM what we have heard, let us learn not to think of the Loss of our Children with a slavish Dread.

IT is to a Parent indeed such a cutting Stroke, that I wonder not if Nature shrink back at the very Mention of it: And, perhaps, it would make those to whom GOD hath denied Children more easy, if they knew what some of the happiest Parents feel in an uncertain Apprehension of the Loss of theirs: An Apprehension which strikes with peculiar Force on the Mind, when Experience hath taught us the Anguish of such an Affliction in former Instances. But let us not anticipate Evils: Perhaps all our Children, who are hitherto spared, may follow us to the Grave Or, if otherwise, we *sorrow not as those who have no Hope*. We may have Reason still to say; *It is well*, and, thro' Divine Grace, we may also have Hearts to say it. Whatever we lose, if we be the Children of GOD, we shall never lose our Heavenly Father, He will still be our Support, and our Joy. And therefore let us turn all our Anxiety about uncertain, future Events, into a holy Solicitude to please him, and to promote religious Impressions in the Hearts of our dear Offspring; that if GOD should see fit to take them away, we may have a Claim to the full Consolations, which I have been representing in the preceding Discourse.

3. LET us not sink in hopeless Sorrow, or break out into clamorous Complaints, if GOD has brought this heavy Affliction upon us.

A STUPID Indifference would be absurd and unnatural: GOD and Man might look upon us as acting a most unworthy Part, should we be like *the Ostrich in the Wilderness, which hardeneth herself against her young ones, as if they were not hers; because GOD hath deprived her of Wisdom, neither hath he imparted to her Understanding*. Let us sorrow like Men, and like Parents; but let us not, in the mean time, forget that we are Christians. Let us remember how common the Calamity is; few Parents are exempt from it; some of the most pious and excellent have lost amiable

Children, with Circumstances perhaps of peculiar Aggravation. 'Tis a Trial which GOD hath chosen for the Exercise of some who have been eminently dear to him, as we may learn from a Variety of Instances both ancient and modern. Let us recollect our many Offences against our heavenly Father, those Sins which such a Dispensation may properly *bring to our Remembrance*; and let that silence us, and teach us to own, that *'tis of the Lord's Mercies we are not consumed*, and that we are *punished less than our Iniquities deserve*. Let us look round on our surviving Comforts; let us look forward to our future, our eternal Hopes; and we shall surely see, that there is still Room for Praise, still a Call for it. Let us review the Particulars mentioned above, and then let Conscience determine whether it doth not become us, in this particular Instance, to say it steadily, and chearfully too, Even *this is well*. And may the GOD of all Grace and Comfort apply these Considerations to our Mind, that we may not only own them, but feel them, as a reviving Cordial when our Heart is overwhelmed within us! In the mean Time, let me beseech you whose *tabernacles are in Peace*, and whose *Children are yet about you*, that you would not be severe in censuring our Tears, till you have experimentally known our Sorrows, and yourselves tasted *the Wormwood and the Gall*, which we, with all our Comforts, must have in a long and a bitter *Remembrance*.

4. LET those of us who are under the Rod, be very solicitous to improve it aright, that in the End it may indeed be *well*.

HEAR, my Brethren, my Friends and Fellow-Sufferers, hear and *suffer the word of Exhortation*. Let us be much concerned, that we may not bear all the Smart of such an Affliction, and, through our own Folly, lose all that Benefit which might, otherwise, be a rich Equivalent. In Proportion to the Grievousness of the Stroke, should be our Care to attend to the Design of it. Let us, now GOD is calling us to Mourning and Lamentation, be *searching and trying our Ways, that we may turn again unto the Lord*. Let us review the Conduct of our Lives, and the State and Tenour of our Affections, that we may observe what hath been deficient, and what irregular; that proper Remedies may be applied, and those important Lessons more thoroughly learnt, which I was mentioning under the former Branch of my Discourse. Let us pray, that through our Tears we may read our Duty, and that by the Heat of the Furnace we may be so melted, that our Dross may be purged away, and the Divine Image instamped on our Souls in brighter and fairer Characters. To sum up all in one Word, let us endeavour to set our Hearts more on that GOD, who is infinitely *better to us than ten Children*, who hath *given us a Name better than that of Sons or of Daughters*, and can abundantly supply the Place of all earthly Enjoyments with the rich Communications of his Grace: Nay, perhaps, we may add, who hath removed some Darling of our Hearts, lest to our infinite Detriment it should fill his Place there, and, by alienating us from his Love and Service, have a fatal Influence on our present Peace, and our future Happiness.

ETERNAL Glory, my Friends, is so great a Thing, and the compleat Love and Enjoyment of GOD so unutterably desirable, that it is well worth our while to bear the sharpest Sorrows, by which we may be more perfectly formed for it. We may even congratulate the Death of our Children, if it bring us nearer to our heavenly Father; and teach us, (instead of filling this Vacancy in our Heart with some new Vanity, which may shortly renew our Sorrows,) to consecrate the whole of it to him who alone deserves, and can alone answer the most intense Affection. Let us try what of this kind may be done. We are now going to the Table of the Lord*, to that very Table where our Vows have often been sealed, where our Comforts have often been reigned, where our *Isaac's* have been conditionally sacrificed, and where we commemorate the real Sacrifice which GOD hath made even of his only begotten Son for us. May our other Sorrows be suspended, while we *mourn for him whom we have pierced, as for an only Son, and are in Bitterness as for a First-born*. From his Blood Consolations spring up, which will flourish even on the Graves of our dear Children; and the Sweetness of that Cup which he there gives us, will temper the most distasteful Ingredients of the other. Our Houses *are not so with GOD*, as they once were, as we once expected they would have been, but *he hath made with us an everlasting Covenant*, and these are the Tokens of it. Blessed be his Name, we hold not the Mercies of that Covenant by so precarious a Tenure as the Life of any Creature. *It is well ordered in all things and sure:* May *it be all our Salvation, and all our Desire*; and then it is but a little while, and all our Complaints will cease. *GOD will wipe away these Tears from our Eyes*, our peaceful and happy Spirits shall ere long meet with those of our Children which he hath taken to himself. Our Bodies shall sleep, and ere long also awake, and arise with theirs. *Death*, that inexorable Destroyer, *shall be swallowed up in Victory*, while we and ours surround the Throne with everlasting Hallelujahs, and own, with another Evidence than we can now perceive; with another Spirit than we can now express, that *All was indeed well.* Amen.

Footnotes.

1. ‡ *The Duke of* Burgundy. *See* Cambray's *Life*, p. 329.
2. * Tibi monstrabo Amatorium sine Medicamento, sine Herbis, sine ullius Veneficæ Carmine, *Si vis amari, ama.* SEN.
3. a Heb. iv. 15.—Heb. ii. 18.
4. b 2 Cor. i. 4.
5. c Job iv. 3,—5.
6. d Job xv. 11.
7. e Isa x. 18.
8. f Heb. xii. 9.
9. g Lev. x. 3.
10. h Job i. 21.
11. i Math. xxi. 16.
12. k Luke i. 18.
13. l Luke i. 38.
14. m Jon. ii. 2.
15. n Jon. iv. 9.
16. o 2 Kings iv. 18, 20.
17. p 1 Kings xvii. 17, & seq.
18. * See *Henry*, in loc.
19. q 1 Tim. vi. 11; 2 Tim. iii. 17.
20. r 2 Kings. iv. 23.
21. s Isa. xxxix. 8.
22. t Ezek. xxiv. 16.
23. u Psal. cxli. 3.
24. w Jer. x. 19.
25. x Psal. lxxiv. 22.
26. y Psal. xxxix. 9.

27. ᶻ 1 Sam. iii. 18.
28. ᵃ Rom. ix. 20.
29. ᵇ Psal ciii. 19.
30. ᶜ Matt. x. 29, 30.
31. ᵈ Psal. cxxi. 4.
32. ᵉ Jer. xv. 7.
33. ᶠ Ezek. xxiv. 16.
34. ᵍ Job xiv. 20.
35. ʰ Psal. xc. 3.
36. ⁱ Job xxi. 22.
37. ᵏ Job. ii. 5.
38. ˡ Psal. xcvii. 2.
39. ᵐ Heb. viii. 10.
40. ⁿ Ibid. xii. 9.
41. ᵒ 2 Cor. i. 3.
42. ᵖ John xviii. 11.
43. ᵠ Eccles. v. 2.
44. ʳ Matt. xxvi. 39.
45. ˢ 2 Sam. xv. 26.
46. ᵗ Rom. viii. 28.
47. ᵘ Rom. iv. 18, 20.
48. ʷ Ibid. viii. 32.
49. ˣ 2 Sam. xix. 28.
50. ʸ Jer. xxxi. 15.
51. ᶻ Prov. xxix. 15.
52. ᵃ Mich. vi. 9.
53. ᵇ Heb. xii. 10.
54. ᶜ Gen. v. 29.
55. ᵈ Jer. ii. 13.

56. ᵉ Psal. xxxix. 7.
57. ᶠ Ibid. xviii. 46.
58. ᵍ 1 Pet. i. 24.
59. ʰ Job xvii. 1.
60. ⁱ Eccles. ix. 10.
61. ᵏ Acts xxiv. 25.
62. ˡ Deu. vi. 7.
63. ᵐ Matth. 21. 16.
64. * *Temple*'s Essays, Vol. I. p. 178.
65. ⁿ Rom. v. 3—5.
66. ᵒ Hab. iii. 17, 18.
67. ᵖ Jonah iv. *ult*.
68. ᵠ 1 Cor. xv. 22.
69. ʳ Gal. iii. 14.
70. ˢ 1 Sam. xxv. 29.
71. ᵗ Rom. xi. 28.
72. ᵗ Psal. cxlv. 9.
73. ᵘ Isa. xxviii. 21.
74. ʷ James v. 11.
75. ˣ Psal. cxi. 4.
76. ʸ Micah vii. 18.
77. ᶻ Isa. xxx. 18.
78. ᵃ Rom. ix. 22.
79. ᵇ Psal. ciii. 14.
80. ᶜ Job xiv. 3.
81. ᵈ Mark x. 13,—16.
82. ᵉ Mat. xviii. 2, 3.
83. ᶠ Rom. viii. 23.
84. ᵍ 1 Cor. xii. 6.

85. ‡ I bless GOD, all these Things were very evident in that dear Child, whose Death occasioned this Discourse.

86. h 1 Cor. xv. 18.

87. i John xiv. 28.

88. * *Howe's* Life, *pag.* 32. *Fal. Edit.*

89. k Isa. xlix. 21.

90. l Philem. *ver.* 13.

91. m 2 Sam. xviii. 33.

92. n Lev. x. 3.

93. * In the Sixth of my *Sermons to young Persons*, intitled, *The Reflections of a pious Parent on the Death of a wicked Child.*

94. p 1 Thess. iv. 13.

95. q Job xxxix. 16, 17.

96. r 1 Kings xvii. 18.

97. s Lam. iii. 22.

98. t Ezra ix. 13.

99. u Job v. 24.

100. w Ibid. xxix. 5.

101. x Lam. iii. 19, 20.

102. y Heb. xiii. 22.

103. z Lam. iii. 40.

104. a 1 Sam. i. 8.

105. b Isa. lvi. 5.

106. * *N. B.* This Sermon was preached *October* 3, 1736. it being Sacrament Day. The Child died *October* 1.

107. c Zech. xii. 10.

108. d 2 Sam. xxiii. 5.

109. e Rev. xxi. 4.

110. f 1 Cor. xv. 54.